IRENAEUS

OF LYONS

THE MAN WHO WROTE BOOKS

HEROES OF THE FAITH

THE BANNER OF TRUTH TRUST

3 Murrayfield Road, Edinburgh EH12 6EL, UK
P.O. Box 621, Carlisle, PA 17013, USA

*

© Sinclair B. Ferguson 2010

*

ISBN-13: 978 1 84871 094 8

*

Typeset in Times New Roman 15/18 at
The Banner of Truth Trust, Edinburgh

Printed in the U.S.A. by
Versa Press, Inc.,
East Peoria, IL

*

IRENAEUS

OF LYONS

THE MAN WHO WROTE BOOKS

SINCLAIR B. FERGUSON

ILLUSTRATED BY ALISON BROWN

THE BANNER OF TRUTH TRUST

CONTENTS

AT THE WRITING TABLE

THE old man sat at his table, writing. He wrote page after page. Sometimes he paused. For a few minutes he seemed to be thinking about something far away, but then he turned back to his writing. He must finish his great book.

He had been planning to write this book for several years now. By the time he had completed it there would be five volumes.

He prayed that God would give him the strength he needed to finish his work.

He had almost reached the end of volume three.

The man's name was Irenaeus (I-ren-ay-us).

MEMORIES

IRENAEUS wrote another sentence, and then paused once more to read over the last words he had written. Why did they make him think of his old friend Florinus? 'Oh, Florinus', he sighed, 'Will you ever read these words?'

He put his pen down. In his imagination he travelled back in time, and covered many miles until he dreamt he was back home in the city of Smyrna as a boy again . . . studying in a classroom.

He was with another boy,
his friend Florinus,
and their teacher.

He remembered what he had thought the first time he had seen Florinus: 'I wonder who that is with the teacher?' It all was as clear in his mind as if it had happened only a week ago. 'Oh, Florinus!' he sighed again.

IRENAUS knew the things he had learned from the teacher had helped him all through his life. 'Yes', he thought, 'that's why I can remember my teenage years more clearly than some of the things that happened last week!' He turned back to his papers and started writing another sentence.

You can tell that this man was a deep thinker, can't you?

What was his story? What was he writing about? And who was the wonderful teacher?

Irenaeus lived in the second century A.D., in the town of Lyons. Lyons was in the area of the Roman Empire called Gaul. Today Lyon (now spelled without an 's') is the second largest city in France. Irenaeus was writing about the gospel. His teacher's name was Polycarp. But when Irenaeus had first met Florinus along with the teacher, they had all been living in Smyrna, many hundreds of miles away.

So why had Irenaeus moved so far away from home?

LIFE IN LYONS

IRENAEUS had become a Christian when he was a boy. He had trusted in Jesus as his Saviour and had given his life to him as his Lord.

His friends in the church in Smyrna had seen how much he wanted to serve Jesus. They had all helped him to do that. They all believed that the Lord was calling Irenaeus to be a missionary church planter in far-away Gaul.

So he came to the city of Lyons and become an elder, or leader, in the church.

A wonderful man called Photinus was the bishop, the minister who led the church. In fact, both Photinus and Irenaeus were church-planting ministers. They loved the Lord Jesus and his people, and they taught them from the Bible.

IT was less than one hundred and fifty years since Jesus had died on the cross and risen again to save his people.

SINCE then, of course, Jesus' disciples had gone all over the world preaching the gospel. Now there were hundreds and hundreds of Christian churches.

THE apostles of Jesus had done something else too.

They had written the New Testament.

PHOTINUS and Irenaeus both loved to preach to the church in Lyons and to teach the message of the New Testament. They would read and then explain passages from the Gospels, or from the Letters of the apostles. Then they would help their friends to understand the meaning of the amazing Book of Revelation written by the Apostle John.

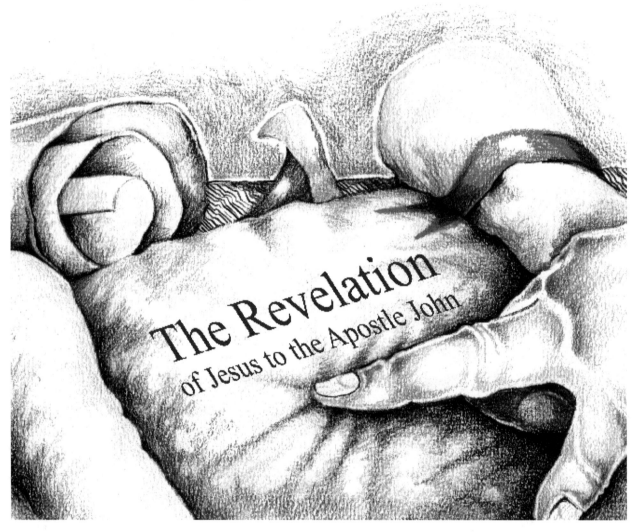

The Christians in Lyons felt that God had really blessed them. They wanted to have Photinus and Irenaeus as their ministers for as long as possible.

THE friends of Irenaeus noticed something special about him. He was very clever. He thought very deeply about the gospel. He was able to understand it. But more than that . . . he was able to explain it very clearly to others.

WHEN there were disagreements about things people could go to Irenaeus to ask him for help. That was important because there were teachers who did not understand the gospel and whose teaching was false.

ONE group of people who were teaching different things from the other churches were called Montanists. They were named after one of their leaders, a man called Montanus. They were starting up their own churches and were upsetting other Christians.

Some people were asking, 'Are the Montanists teaching what God's Word says, or are they not? Are they right, or are they wrong?'

Whenever Irenaeus was asked that kind of question, he would give a little smile, and then say quietly, 'Well, what do the Scriptures say about this?'

That was a good answer.

IRENAEUS GOES TO ROME

THE bishop in the church at Rome, whose name was Eleutherus, decided that he should ask other bishops to send one of their best ministers to a conference where they could agree together on what the Bible really taught.

Who do you think was chosen to go from Lyons?
Yes, it was Irenaeus.

So Irenaeus set out on the long journey from Lyons to Rome, the capital city of the Roman Empire.

He met bishop Eleutherus and many other Christian leaders.

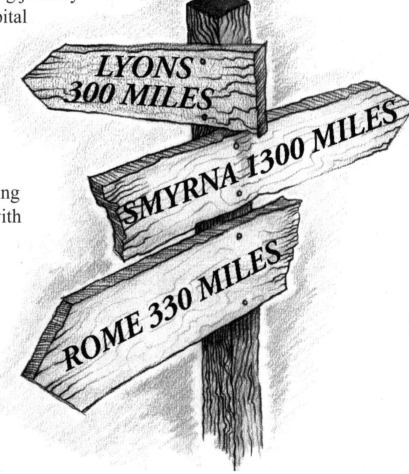

IT must have been an amazing experience for him to be with the other ministers.

Everyone saw how well he understood the gospel. Perhaps some of them may even have said to him, 'Irenaeus, you need to write a book to help us and all of the churches!'

AT the end of the conference Irenaeus returned to his home in Lyons.

BUT something had happened while he was away . . .

The Roman Emperors did not want to trust Jesus, or have him as their own Lord, and they did not like Christians.

They were afraid that members of Jesus' kingdom might be their enemies. So they sometimes tried to destroy the church.

The Roman Emperors were very clever. They knew that the best way to destroy the church was by getting rid of its leaders. That was what had happened in Lyons.

BISHOP Photinus, Irenaeus's dear friend, had been accused of not obeying the Emperor. He had been tried by the Romans. He was found guilty and then put to death.

THE enemies of Jesus thought that if they could get rid of the ministers then the Christians would scatter.

BISHOP Photinus had believed that if the Roman authorities made him a martyr, the Lord Jesus would give his church another bishop. He was sure he knew who that would be. So he had died, trusting the Lord Jesus to keep building the church in Lyons.

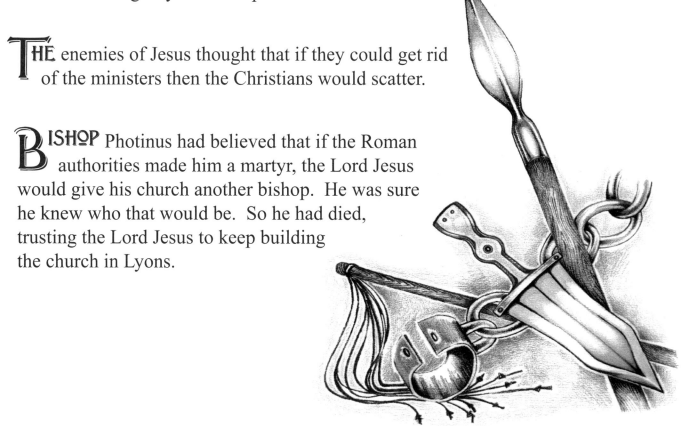

SOME of the church members became so frightened that they turned away from following the Lord Jesus.

But others stood firm and became even stronger.

THE Christians in Lyons were very sad that Photinus had suffered. But they knew he had gone to be with the Lord Jesus. They did not stop following the Lord.

And they decided that the Lord had already given them their next bishop.

Yes, it was Irenaeus!

CAN you imagine what Irenaeus must have felt like when he was told that he was to take the place of his friend who had just been killed?

He prayed like this:

'Heavenly Father, you have given me these great honours.
First you gave me new life through your Son, Jesus.
Then you gave me a great teacher in Smyrna.
Then you gave me bishop Photinus, a wonderful friend who gave his all for you.
And now you have called me to take care of the people my friend loved.
They are your sheep.
I will serve you with all my strength.
I love them and am willing to be their bishop.'

AND so Irenaeus became the bishop of Lyons.

IRENAEUS SPEAKS ABOUT THE CREATOR

SHEPHERDS do two things. They feed their sheep, and they protect their sheep. Bishops, who are spiritual shepherds, do the same thing for their flock of Christian believers.

IRENAEUS did both of these things by teaching his congregation from the Word of God, the Bible. He had a very interesting way of preaching the gospel of Jesus, from the beginning of Genesis right to the end of the Book of Revelation.

SOMETIMES he explained the gospel to the congregation like this . . .

'OUR God, who created the world and everything in it, is a good and wonderful heavenly Father. He lovingly sent his Son Jesus into the world to be our Saviour.

'Then, when the Lord Jesus had gone back to heaven, the Holy Spirit of God was sent to help us to follow Jesus. This is how we know that the one, true and living God is three persons: the Father, the Son and the Holy Spirit.

'You can think of it this way, my dear friends . . .

'The Son and the Spirit worked like the two hands of God. The Father planned everything; then the Son and the Spirit completed everything the Father planned.'

'GOD made the heavens above us, the sun and moon, the stars and everything we see in the sky . . . the birds, the butterflies, the bees, and all the creatures that fly. He made all the animals in the world.

'He made the mountains and rivers, the trees, the fruit, the grass, the lakes and the seas. He made the earth for us to enjoy. When he made everything, he made it good!'

IRENAEUS had an important reason for saying that God made everything good. That is what the Bible teaches.

BUT some teachers were saying that anything you could see, or touch (what they called 'matter'), is evil and bad. Only what you could not see or touch (what they called 'spirit'), could be good.

Some of these teachers believed that since our world is 'matter' it must be evil. They thought it must have been created by a lesser god than the great God. In fact some people who knew little about Jesus were teaching that the god who had made the world was different from the heavenly Father who sent the Lord Jesus to save us!

'NO! No! No!' said Irenaeus. 'That is all wrong!'
The Christians in Lyons did not often hear Irenaeus raise his voice loudly. But he did when he said this!

'IF only people knew the Bible better. The truth is all perfectly plain there!' said Irenaeus to himself. He was determined that his congregation would know the truth that Jesus had taught. So he continued to teach them:

'Why is this world the way it is? Why do things go wrong? Why do people do bad things to themselves and to others?

'GOD has given us the answer right at the beginning of his Word, the Bible!

'God made everything good. God made the world for his glory.

'But he also made the world as a home for the greatest of all his creations: man and woman. God the Father, the Son and the Holy Spirit agreed that they would make people like us. What an amazing idea!

'More than that, God decided to make the first two people, called Adam and Eve, like himself.'

GOD MADE US IN HIS IMAGE

IRENAEUS looked down at his Old Testament and put his finger on some words that he said very slowly.

He repeated them.

Then he repeated them again.

'Try to memorise these words', he said to the congregation . . .

'Then God said, "Let us make man in our image, after our likeness. And let them have dominion over the fish of the sea and over the birds of the heavens and over the livestock and over all the earth and over every creeping thing that creeps on the earth." So God created man in his own image, in the image of God he created him; male and female he created them. And God blessed them. And God said to them, "Be fruitful and multiply and fill the earth and subdue it and have dominion over the fish of the sea and over the birds of the heavens and over every living thing that moves on the earth."'*

_____

* These words are from Genesis chapter 1 verses 26-28.

IRENAEUS paused as he spoke. There were more words he wanted to read, but he felt so much thankfulness in his heart to God that he had to stand still for a moment, saying nothing.

Then he added: 'Dear friends, listen to what God's Word then says . . .

'"And God saw everything that he had made, and" . . . do you see? . . . "it was very good."

'DON'T you see that everything our heavenly Father made was originally perfectly good? He even made us as his image. He made us like himself . . . good and holy, true and loving.

'He was so generous that he put Adam and Eve in a beautiful garden called the Garden of Eden.

'"Look after this garden for me and make it even bigger", God said.

'THEN something terrible happened . . .'

SOMETHING GOES WRONG

'**G**OD wanted Adam and Eve to love, trust and obey him just because he is a loving heavenly Father. He had made them holy, loving, and good by nature. But he wanted them to be holy, loving, and good by their own choice as well. He wanted them to grow strong in trusting and serving him. So he gave them a simple challenge.

'**G**OD told them that there was one tree in the garden that they should avoid. They must not eat its fruit. God gave the tree a name: "The tree of the knowledge of good and evil."'

IRENAEUS continued, sadness filling his eyes . . . 'But you know what happened. The Devil tempted them to eat from this tree. Instead of using their ears to listen to what God had said, they went only by what they could see with their eyes. The fruit looked and smelled delicious. They ate it.'

IRENAEUS wondered if he should explain this to his congregation.

Why did God make such delicious-looking fruit and then tell Adam and Eve not to eat it?

He knew the answer. Everything God makes is good! There was no poison in the fruit!

If the tree had looked horrible, and its fruit had looked poisonous, Adam and Eve would simply have said, 'Ugh, that looks horrible, let's avoid it.'

The tree was a real test of whether they would listen to what God said. Would they trust, love, and obey him because he was God? Would they trust him as their Father?

'I will tell them about that another time', thought Irenaeus.

'Some other day I will help them to understand how the Devil used a snake to tempt them. But today the most important thing is that I explain all about the Lord Jesus.'

IRENAEUS continued his teaching . . .

'So you see, our foolish parents disobeyed God. They began to live by what they could see with their eyes instead of what they had heard with their ears. They turned away from God's Word.

'God had made Adam and Eve to be king and queen over the earth.

'So, when they disobeyed, sinned and fell, everything began to go wrong.'

EVERYTHING GOES WRONG

'**B**ECAUSE we have all come from Adam and Eve, we are all members of their family; there is something wrong with each of us right from the very beginning. That is why the beloved Apostle Paul wrote that "all have sinned and fall short of the glory of God."*

'This is why we do not love God, and why we do not love each other as we should. This is why our world is so full of evil, why bad things happen, and why there is so much sadness and sorrow.

'This world was created good. It was created by the heavenly Father. We are the ones who have spoiled it! The real problem is our sin! This is the bad news the Bible tells us. But . . .'

AS the Christians watched Irenaeus and listened eagerly to what he was saying, his expression suddenly changed. The lines on his face seemed to disappear, the sadness in his voice was gone. He lifted up his head. He lifted up his arms. And then he exclaimed with joy . . .

---

* Romans chapter 3 verse 23.

'BUT, my dear, dear friends, there is good news, wonderful news! When we begin to understand what has gone wrong, we will be amazed by what our heavenly Father has done to save us! This is why the gospel is such good news!

'LISTEN, my friends, to what the beloved Apostle John taught . . .

"GOD so loved the world . . ."

'Yes', added Irenaeus, 'God loved this world full of sinful men and women, boys and girls like us . . . "that he gave his only Son, so that whoever believes in him should not perish but have eternal life."*

'LET me tell you', Irenaeus continued, 'the story of how God sent us a Saviour.

'GOD made the world good. He created the first man, Adam, and gave him a garden. God told him to look after the earth for his glory. He also told Adam to show his love for God by promising not to eat of one special tree in the garden.'

---

* These words come from John's Gospel, chapter 3 verse 16.

'BUT Adam disobeyed God's command. He sinned. He brought sin into the world and he ruined it. He deserved to be punished for his sin. And because we are all members of Adam's family we have become sinners too.

'DO you see the problem?' asked Irenaeus. 'How can we be allowed to stand in God's presence again? Adam, and you and I have all sinned.

'We need someone to take our place and obey God for us!

'And what else would he need to do for us?

'He would need to take the punishment we all deserve for our sin!
None of us could ever do these things — for we are all sinners too.'

THEN Irenaeus smiled again.

'BUT GOD has solved the problem!
He sent his Son into the world.
Jesus has done what we cannot do!
He has obeyed God the Father in our place.
And he has died for our sins on the cross.

'DO you see?
Jesus is the Second Adam who saves us!
And he did it at another tree — on Mount Calvary!'

25

'THERE he took the penalty we deserved. He died for our sins, and he defeated our enemy the Devil. Then in his resurrection he defeated death.

'Now, through the gift of the Holy Spirit he gives us new and eternal life!

'One day he will return and renew the whole creation. Then, once more, like Adam and Eve were supposed to, all of us who belong to the Lord Jesus will reign with him!'

IRENAEUS was almost finished his teaching now. He went on for another few minutes . . .

'Learn the story of the two Adams. It is the greatest story in the world because it is the story of the world! Learn this story, my friends! Trust in the Second Adam, our Lord Jesus, our Saviour. He changes everything. And at the end, all will be well.'

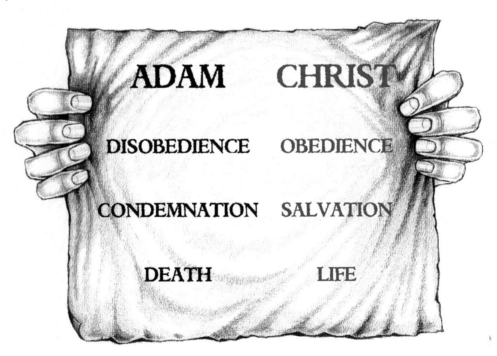

IRENAEUS paused again. Once more he smiled at the people who were listening to him. He knew they loved him as much as he loved them.

SOME of them had become Christians only recently. This was the first time they had heard Irenaeus explain things this way. They smiled back, like people who had discovered hidden treasure.

One or two of the older people had other thoughts in their minds as Irenaeus finished his sermon . . . They were thinking:

'DEAR Irenaeus, he loves to tell us about the two Adams. It thrills him so much. Some of us have heard it now dozens of times. It makes the Bible story so simple and clear. We love it when Irenaeus tells us about the promise God gave to Adam and Eve, that someone from their family line would conquer the Devil, even though he would be hurt himself.*

'We love it when he tells us about the great battle that has been fought throughout history between the Devil and the people of God. It is all so simple, and yet it is also so deep. And it also helps us to understand what it means to live today as Christians when the enemies of Jesus do terrible things . . . as they did to Photinus.

'WHAT a privilege it is to have Irenaeus as our bishop! Every time he tells this simple story he still seems to be thrilled by it. What a wonderful gospel we have! Our children are beginning to understand this story and are trusting in the Lord Jesus as their Saviour too. And at the same time our clever bishop, Irenaeus, seems to feel he can never get to the bottom of the wonders of God's grace!'

_____
* This promise is found in Genesis chapter 3 verse 15.

A LETTER TO FLORINUS

AS if he had wakened up from a dream, Irenaeus's eyes focused again on the pages on his writing table.

He knew that even while he had been day-dreaming, something was troubling him. Now he remembered what it was.

It was his old friend Florinus!

What had happened to him since the last time they had been together?

He had heard that Florinus had been led astray from the Christian faith and from the church by some of these false teachers. Could that really be true?

IRENAEUS pushed away the page on which he had been writing. He had thought often about doing something, but had never done it.

He must do it today!
He must write to Florinus.

IN the time of Irenaeus people usually began their letters by mentioning first the writer and then the person who was going to receive it.

SO Irenaeus wrote . . .

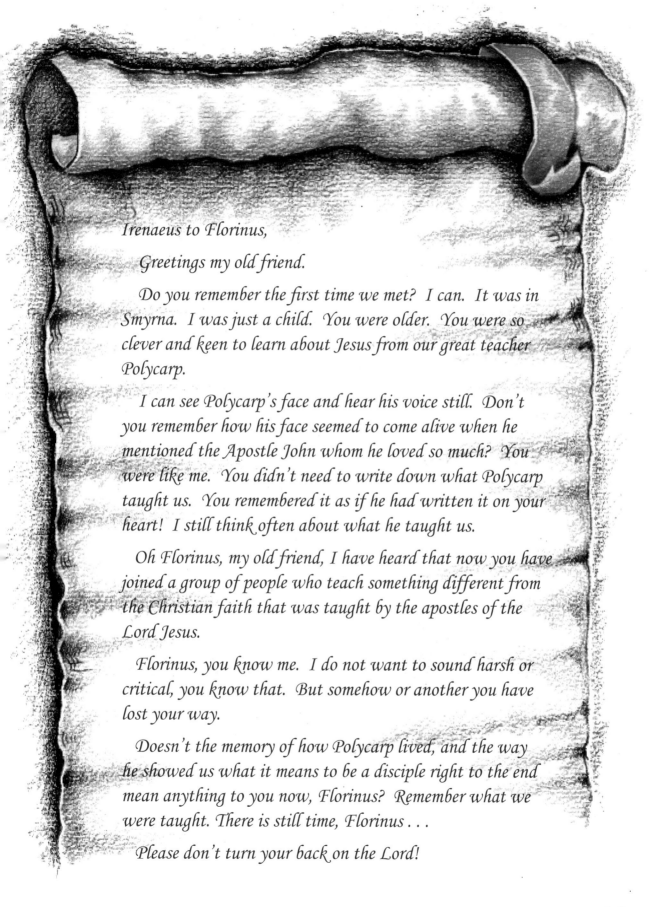

Irenaeus to Florinus,

Greetings my old friend.

Do you remember the first time we met? I can. It was in Smyrna. I was just a child. You were older. You were so clever and keen to learn about Jesus from our great teacher Polycarp.

I can see Polycarp's face and hear his voice still. Don't you remember how his face seemed to come alive when he mentioned the Apostle John whom he loved so much? You were like me. You didn't need to write down what Polycarp taught us. You remembered it as if he had written it on your heart! I still think often about what he taught us.

Oh Florinus, my old friend, I have heard that now you have joined a group of people who teach something different from the Christian faith that was taught by the apostles of the Lord Jesus.

Florinus, you know me. I do not want to sound harsh or critical, you know that. But somehow or another you have lost your way.

Doesn't the memory of how Polycarp lived, and the way he showed us what it means to be a disciple right to the end mean anything to you now, Florinus? Remember what we were taught. There is still time, Florinus . . .

Please don't turn your back on the Lord!

'DEAR Polycarp', Irenaeus often thought. 'What a wonderful bishop of Smyrna you were! What a teacher you were to Florinus and me! What an example of a disciple of Jesus!

'I can still remember you telling us about your friend bishop Ignatius of Antioch and his faithfulness to the Lord Jesus.

'You used to smile when you mentioned his name and remind us that it came from the Latin word *ignis* meaning "fire". Yes, you used to say he was "Fire by name, and on fire for Jesus by grace."

'You did not know that behind your back we used to say, "Polycarp comes from two Greek words: *polus* meaning "much" and *karpos* meaning "fruit". You were "Much fruit" by name, and much fruit by grace!'

IRENAEUS sighed once more. Now that he had finished his letter to Florinus he turned again to the pages of his great book.

'Where was I now?' he asked. He looked at the pages he had already written.

IRENAEUS AND HIS BOOK

IRENAEUS thought again about what he was going to call his book. 'I am not very good at giving my books the kind of titles that will make people want to read them!', he thought. 'Well, I will just use a title that tells people what my book is all about.' So he took another piece of paper, and on it he wrote the words . . .

IN his book he had described all kinds of false beliefs. Some of them were very strange indeed. 'Why do people believe such foolish things?' he wondered. 'Sadly, if they will not believe in the true God, and in the Saviour Jesus, they will make up all kinds of things to believe.'

HE looked again at the word 'Against'. 'That doesn't sound very welcoming', he thought. 'But the loving Lord Jesus taught us that we should not welcome false teaching. He told us that false teachers would appear, and that they would lead people astray. The Apostles John, and Peter and Paul all saw the results of false teaching. They taught that it was even more dangerous than persecution. Persecution can hurt our bodies for a little while. False teaching can hurt our souls for ever.'

'I think I will keep my title!' Irenaeus said out loud. 'But I must take time to write about how wonderful the true gospel of Jesus is, and what a wonderful heavenly Father we can come to know and love through him. And, yes, I must write too about how the Holy Spirit changes our hearts and our lives!'

AND so Irenaeus went back to work. When he was not busy teaching and preaching and caring for his congregation and sending letters, he would take out his book and write more. Sometimes he worked late into the night.

Irenaeus wrote more than one book but this was the biggest one.

Eventually he finished it. He arranged all the pages together in order. And then, on top of the pile, he placed the page on which he had written the title.

IRENAEUS had heard people say to him:

'Teaching that doesn't agree with the Bible isn't really so bad, is it?'

But as he looked at his great book, he remembered the words of the Lord Jesus, 'Whoever is not with me is against me . . .'*

So he decided to keep the title exactly as he had written it: *Against All False Teaching.*

Little did he know that all round the world Christians would read his great book.

And little did he know that they would continue to think about the wonderful way he told the story of the Father's good creation, man's tragic sin, Jesus' great salvation, the Holy Spirit's life-changing power, and how history would end in the triumph of God.

---

* Matthew chapter 12 verse 30.

THE New Testament tells us that the Lord Jesus Christ gives his people different kinds of gifts. His church is like a body with hands and feet, with eyes and ears, with a mind and a mouth. Each of us helps to make the body work properly. We do not all have the same gifts.

ONE of the gifts Jesus gives to his people is the ability to understand the gospel well, being able to teach it clearly, and to warn about the dangers of false teaching. These teachers must have a loving concern for people and for their salvation.

These are the gifts God gives to ministers, to elders, and others.

IRENAEUS had these gifts. He used them well.

WE still need Christians with these gifts today because it is so important for us to understand the teaching of the Lord Jesus.

WILL you pray that the Lord Jesus Christ will work in the hearts of those he calls to be teachers and preachers. Pray that Jesus will help them, and fill them with faith and with love for God and for his people, and help them to understand the gospel . . . just as he did in the life of Irenaeus, bishop of the church in Lyons?

ABOUT IRENAEUS OF LYONS

Irenaeus of Lyons – The Man who Wrote Books is a true story.

Irenaeus was born around 130 A.D. or 140 A.D. in the province of the Roman Empire called Asia Minor. He seems to have grown up in a Christian family and belonged to the Christian church in Smyrna, which is now the city of Izmir in Turkey.

When he was a young man, God called him to serve as a minister of the gospel.

The church in Smyrna sent him to the city of Lyons in the Roman Province of Gaul. In those days Lyons (now known as Lyon, in France) had a population of about 50,000 people. Irenaeus lived in Lyons from about 170 A.D. to about 200 A.D.

Irenaeus served the church in Lyons with great enthusiasm. They wrote about him that he was 'zealous for the covenant of Christ'.

In his earlier life Irenaeus was taught by Polycarp, the minister of the church in Smyrna. Polycarp became his life-long hero. You can read more about Polycarp in *Polycarp of Smyrna — The Man whose Faith Lasted*. Polycarp lived at the same time as Ignatius of Antioch. You can read about him in *Ignatius of Antioch — The Man who Faced Lions*.

Irenaeus died around the year 200 A.D.

HEROES OF THE FAITH

HEROES OF THE FIRST CENTURIES	HEROES OF THE TRUTH	HEROES OF THE DARKNESS AND THE DAWN	HEROES OF THE REFORMATION

IGNATIUS ?-117
POLYCARP 70-156
   IRENAEUS 130/40-200

      ATHANASIUS 296-373
       BASIL OF CAESAREA 329-379
      GREGORY OF NYSSA 330-395
     GREGORY OF NAZIANZUS 330-389
       AUGUSTINE 354-430

           GOTTSCHALK 805-869
          ANSELM 1033-1109
            JOHN WYCLIFFE 1329-84
             JAN HUSS 1373-1415

                  MARTIN LUTHER 1483-1546
                 WILLIAM TYNDALE 1494-1536
                   JOHN CALVIN 1509-64
                    JOHN KNOX 1514-72

BIRTH OF JESUS
B.C./A.D.
1/1---100--200-----300----400------------1100------------1400------------1500------------

Timeline

WILLIAM PERKINS 1558-1602
JOHN OWEN 1616-83
JOHN BUNYAN 1628-88

JOHN WESLEY 1703-92
JONATHAN EDWARDS 1703-1758
GEORGE WHITEFIELD 1714-1770

WILLIAM WILBERFORCE 1759-1833
WILLIAM CAREY 1761-1834
HENRY MARTYN 1781-1812
JOHN G. PATON 1824-1907

C. H. SPURGEON 1834-92
D. M. LLOYD-JONES 1899-1981

------1600-----------1700--------------------------------1800------------1900-----------------2000

A Personal Word to Parents About Heroes of the Faith

Many of our children enjoy having heroes, but they are living in a world that encourages them instead to have 'idols'.

Sometimes, perhaps, the difference is simply a choice of words. But today it is usually more. For the 'idols' our children are encouraged to have — whether by media coverage or peer pressure — are to be 'adored' not because of their character, but because of their image.

By contrast a 'hero' is someone who is much more than a 'personality' about whom we may know little or nothing. A hero is someone who has shown moral fibre, who has overcome difficulties and opposition, who has been tested and has stood firm.

This series is about such people — heroes of the Christian faith — whose lives remind us of the words of Hebrews 13:7: 'Consider the outcome of their way of life, and imitate their faith.'

There are different kinds of heroes. The books in this series reflect the fact that some become heroes by being willing to die for Christ; others because of how they served the church of Christ; yet others because of what they taught about Christ; and others because of where they were prepared to go for Christ.

The HEROES OF THE FAITH books are intended to build up into a kind of church family album — pictures of those who, throughout the centuries, have been members of the family of God.

Many of us who are parents wish we could teach our children more about the story of the church, to help them see the privilege of belonging to a spiritual family that stretches back over the centuries and extends to the ends of the earth. This series aims to cover the centuries-long story of the church and to introduce children to heroes of the faith in every period of history.

None of these heroes was perfect — they all recognised their need of the Lord Jesus Christ as their Saviour and Lord. None of them claimed perfect understanding or perfect obedience. But each of them aimed to love the Lord with heart and mind and soul and strength. In that sense they were true heroes.

Many of these heroes were ministers and preachers of the gospel of Jesus Christ. But they were not heroes simply because they were ministers. The word 'minister' means 'servant'. They were people who became leaders in the church; they became heroes because they were servants both of the Lord Jesus and of his people.

I count it a privilege to have the opportunity of introducing your family, and especially your children, to these HEROES OF THE FAITH. May they become heroes too!

SINCLAIR B. FERGUSON

40